FUNNY AND IRONIC

AMAZING, HAPPY AND FEEL GOOD STORIES

MARCO DI NOIA

Funny and Ironic Amazing, Happy and Feel Good Stories

tellwell

Tellwell Talent
www.tellwell.ca

ISBN
978-0-2288-5406-7 (Paperback)

DEDICATION

Thank you to Frangipani House for the staff and friendly people that create an environment that is conducive for writing stories and dedicated to people suffering from depression who like to read happy, ironic, funny, amazing, and feel-good stories to make them forget their problems and ease their depression. I hope everyone with depression gets better.

If you don't have depression, consider how lucky you are, and you can get enjoyment and feel happy from reading this book and a laugh as well.

AN INTRODUCTION INTO MARCO'S HUMOUR

I am a bit funny at times.

I have made people laugh and they like talking to me.

I have a silly sense of humour and it is easier to be silly and humorous than to always have an intelligent humour.

Silly is not an intelligent humour, but it makes you laugh more because I am not trying to show off my intelligence.

It is a little bit stupid but funny at the same time.

That is what silly means.

A silly humour is not trying to be better than others with your high intelligence, just funny.

When you are being silly, you can laugh at yourself while making others laugh.

When making intelligent humour, you can only wait to see if others laugh at what you say.

With silly humour you both laugh together.

My stories are a bit silly but funny with a lot of intelligent humor thrown in for good mix.

But you also need some intelligent humour mixed in with the silliness.

And my humour has a good mixture of both.

If I've got my friends around me who I can talk to, I can make them laugh and that would make us happy at least for a while.

CONTENTS OF STORIES

INTRODUCTION – A CHOICE OF A FEW FUNNY SHORT STORIES

Writing stories helped me with my depression, I wrote these funny short stories to help me deal with boredom and they made me laugh. These stories could be conversation starters and could be read at a party or gathering and people can make comments.

It would be stretching my brain too far to write one hundred stories. I can think of some funny bits I have already written; they make me laugh and they might make you chuckle too. Like the zookeepers who found a job in the Air Force and now dispatches missiles. Or the girl bungee jumping in a dress and G-string, or the streaker who put his clothes back on and left the building. There are the stories about: the astronauts who were left to wander the Universe for eternity, and the horse who had his stripes painted on like a zebra, and the monkey who packed his bags and moved back to Africa, and the aliens who survived their crash landing and are walking the Earth today. These are just a few of the stories that make me laugh and there are many more!

FIGHTING IN THE ZOO

Yesterday, Marco and his friends went to the zoo. My favourite animal the Gorilla was having a fight, what a sight! The Gorilla was massive with huge shoulder, chest, and arm muscles. He was 6 foot 8" tall. Having a fight with the Ox. The Ox was fat and almost as big as a Horse. They were fighting, guess who won? The Gorilla got the Ox by the long and sharp horns and the Ox flipped the Gorilla and the zookeepers hosed them down with ice cold water. So, the Ox and the Gorilla teamed up and the Gorilla RRROAAARRREEEDDD! And the zookeepers threw bananas at them and then RAN!

Epilogue: The zookeepers lost their jobs at the zoo [sad face] but, next week got new jobs at the Air Force where they dispatched missiles.

FROM ZERO TO HERO

Once upon a time there was a man who was tough, tougher than Hercules.

He was a caveman because he was homeless. He wore ragged old clothes and had dreadlocks for hair.

He was tough because he was homeless. He lived in a cave and had little sleep.

He had no money, he lost it on the horses and had no job to earn back his money.

One day it rained, and he saw a car smash, he rescued a woman from the smash. She was rich, filthy rich, but then all her money got siphoned out of her bank account from a scammer.

They became homeless together.

As a manly man, he tracked down the robber and handed him to the police.

He was rewarded $10,000.

They bought a camper van and set up a drink stall outside the army base, for the soldiers who came by thirsty, they drank and ate meat pies. Enabling the couple to save up and buy a house and they lived happily ever after.

THE ZOO ESCAPEE'S

The Tiger, the Giraffe, the elephant, the crocodile, and the Zebra.

They all escaped from the zoo.

They were being transported to another zoo and the truck turned over because it was going to fast around a corner in bad windy weather. There was a lightning bolt to the trucks lock and set it on fire. With a loud bang there was lot of smoke and the animals were scared.

The fire caused all the animals to be released or they would have been burnt to death, so they escaped. Marco got out of the truck. Marco yelled "it's a tense situation, with all the animals getting away."

Marco's ingenious idea to capture the animals, he hitched a ride on the zebra's back.

Marco and the zebra ran over to the giraffe, climbed up his neck. Pulled out his binoculars where he spotted the elephant.

He instructed the giraffe to run faster! and caught up to the elephant.

Then jumped on the elephant's back. The elephant called out to Marco, "I can see the flashing stripes of the tiger, in the distance."

Tiger said, "you found me!!!" But the crocodile is belly crawling towards the ocean. But there was a great white shark showing his large white teeth.

And the crocodile was scared back on to the land.

The animals where frightened by their running romp.

And they all agreed that they would be relocated to the African Lion Safari Park in Australia.

The giraffe said, "as long as there are no wild and hungry animals out there." "You will be separated from the lions with better food." Marco replied, "they are all tamed and friendly like yourselves" Suddenly, all the animals rushed into the replacement truck with gusto.

THE FIREWORKS WELCOMING IN THE NEW YEAR

The fireworks exploded with their brightness in the night sky.

It was as loud as thunder and lightning.

Some of the designs displayed when the fireworks went off were like chariots unloading their explosives.

The fireworks filled the sky with a blast of drums.

Boom! Boom! Boom! The sound of music was turned off.

And the explosive, thunderous noise of the fireworks filled everyone's ears.

People shouted with joy welcoming in the New Year.

HAPPY NEW YEAR!!!

GREEDY OLD MAN

The old man was greedy, he could not get enough money from the lotto. He won $7000 in the second division, but he wanted to double it --- no triple it!

He placed the $7000 as a bet on a 2 to 1 favourite at the TAB in Paramatta and he lost all his money.

When he got home, he said to his wife "Honey I lost all the money," his wife beat him "That money was supposed to be for a holiday!" She screamed and she punched him in the eye and kicked him in the thigh "That'll teach you, for putting all your money on one horse."

The next day Marco saw the old man on the street with a black eye and said: "That'll teach you, to put all your money on one horse, you should have put $20 on 20 races and enjoyed your day at the TAB you loser!"

THE INJURED HORSE THAT WON

One day, Marco and his friend Wendy went to the racecourse. In the stables they saw an injured horse who was lying on straw and they felt sorry for him, so they gave him a mystery injection.

The syringe has an amber coloured liquid, something that bodybuilders used for muscle strength and recovery.

In the race, the horses were snorting and blowing air through their nostrils, their mouths had foam and they were sweating.

Marco and Wendy enjoyed the race, as they watched the beautiful chestnut-coloured horse run faster than every other horse and win.

"We're having such great fun!". "The horse won; must be the mystery injection we gave him!" Marco said.

Afterwards Marco and Wendy went to Frangipani house and told the story about the horse.

Marco said he had shares in the horse and bet on him. Everyone praised Marco and Wendy and thanked them for their good deed.

That night Marco and Wendy slept well. Marco dreamt about the Melbourne Cup.

THE SUPER HORSE

If there was a horse that could swim faster than he could run, then you could take him to the beach and ride him in the surf.

There was a big horse, who was shiny and black, with a jet-black mane. This horse loved to rescue people and wanted to join the lifeguards.

The lifeguards wanted this horse as a rescue horse. He could run on the sand yet could swim faster than he could run.

If you were swimming and saw a shark, the shark would never catch you, with the horse of course.

There was a shark, and of course, the horse was not scared for obvious reasons, and the horse ran on the sand and swam out to a boy and rescued him from the shark. He was a super horse. WHAT A HORSE!

SINGLES' HOLIDAY IN NEW ZEALAND

Marco won a large amount of money on the Melbourne Cup, so he went on a holiday to New Zealand in the summer to get away from the Sydney heatwave. He was hoping to meet a nice lady on the singles' holiday tour, and he met a lady with a funny accent. It was a Kiwi accent. She was a ginger-haired and green-eyed lady and Marco thought her accent was funny, especially when she ordered the 'fush and chups'. She thought Marco's stories were hilarious, especially the one about the monkey and told him to write more. They fell in love; she came back to Australia and they got married.

HOLIDAY IN BYRON BAY

On a holiday in Byron Bay, where the water is cool and the air is warm,

I swim and lay on the beach with scenery to look at.

The scenery of a lighthouse and waves splashing onto the rocks.

And dolphins swimming alongside the surfers.

When I swim with the dolphins, I feel peace and tranquillity.

And meeting a nice lady to keep me company.

I would tell her funny stuff and make her laugh.

THE STUPID MONKEY

Marco was skipping down the street with a song in his ears.

A fat monkey, who had black hair and a double chin (cheeky looking), came swinging from a nearby tree and threw a banana onto the footpath in Marco's direction.

Someone yelled, "Marco get out the way!" but it was too late, Marco slipped over and broke his ankle.

The monkey laughed stupidly, Marco was fuming and wanted revenge.

The next day Marco shot the monkey with a slug gun.

The monkey packed his bags and moved back to the African jungle.

THE RETURN OF THE MONKEY

Marco finished his slugs for his slug gun because he wasted them on the rhinoceros and elephants at the Zoo. The monkey returned from Africa to seek vengeance on Marco, the monkey was wearing a jock strap to hold up his pants, his gut sticks out.

He came back with a hundred banana skins; he had eaten them all and become fat. He threw them all at Marco in a fit of rage! So, Marco kicked him in the leg and broke his ankle and the monkey could not get up because he was too fat.

Marco put him in a wheelchair and took him to hospital and the monkey recovered and they became best friends. When Marco got sick and went to hospital the Monkey visited him. Marco adopted the Monkey as a pet.

HALLOWEEN NIGHT

It was midnight on the eve of Halloween and the witches, ghosts and ghouls came out to play.

The witches were planning to cook Marco—the local Wizard because they were jealous of his majestic skills—and make him into delicious candy for the trick-or-treaters.

Jerry the Ghost told Marco of the witches' plans.

Marco saw some good in Jerry the ghost and converted him to pass over to the other side, Heaven. Marco showed Jerry the basics in the Bible and told him he needed to ask for forgiveness for committing suicide.

The witches made a brew in a large pot and filled it with sugar, honey, and water. The rats were waiting eagerly next to the pot hoping for something drastic to happen. The witches picked up the steaming hot brew by the rim and as they went to pour it into the candy mould, the witches slipped and spilt the brew. The salivating rats exuberantly drank the sweet spilt brew.

Marco was spared from being boiled in the brew and Jerry the ghost passed over to the other side and the dawn woke everyone up.

THE HORSE AND THE JACKASS

The horse jumped around like a jackass

and the jackass ran fast like a horse

and the mule didn't know which one to be friends with

a horse that jumped like a jackass or a jack ass that ran fast like a horse

then the butcher came out and looked at the three of them and said, "there's some mighty good horse flesh out there."

The horse and the jackass ran fast, and the mule bolted.

THUNDER AND LIGHTNING AT THE CRICKET

The cricket ball comes thundering down from the bowlers' hand and it's the batsman who has to strike at it.

With a crack, it goes all the way for a six and flies into the crowd

The crowd roars and another six is required of the last ball.

The bowler comes in again with a lightning bolt.

And the batsman slashes at it.

But the stumps are broken, and the bowler wins the jewel between bat and ball.

And the bowler gets the glory of the wicket, and the team celebrates their victory.

All go to the pub afterwards and the bowler shouts the batsman a beer and the batsman burps out, "that lightning bolt of a ball was too good to hit for six."

THE MAGICAL APPLECADO TREE

The scientists were trying to create hybrid fruits and vegetables for more deliciousness when they created the magical Applecado tree.

There was a magical tree that was full of fruit. When you ate the Applecado's, you got as high as a kite.

The scientists had crossed an apple tree with an avocado tree and created a magical Applecado tree.

One day, the Applecado got converted into injections by the drug companies.

Sean signed up to be the first to get it. Marco got jealous and bought seeds from the Applecado tree so he could sell them on the black market to make a profit.

The FBI saw that he was making too much money and they decided to double his medications and dumped him in the hospital where he got depressed, so they gave him the Applecado injection, and he got better and forgot about the magical tree and got out of hospital.

THE ZEBRA, THE LION AND THE CROCODILE

In the woods, in Africa, there was a log.

The zebra came and sat on the log because he was tired.

Then the lion came and sat on the log.

Then a crocodile came and sat on the log under the tree.

They all began to talk about how hot it was, and it was good to rest in the shade on the log.

When the night came, and the cool arrived.

The zebra fell asleep.

The lion and the crocodile stayed awake with hunger, realising it was days since they had eaten.

They did not want to fight each other.

But they argued about who deserved to eat the zebra.

They could not come to an agreement, so they both savaged the zebra in his sleep.

INTO THE UNIVERSE, THERE IS A GOD

In the galaxy, there was a starship called the Supernova. It was on a voyage to the outer limits of the universe, in search of intelligent life, the possible existence of God and the beginning of the universe and the Throne of God. One day in the tenth year of the voyage, a strange and loud voice could be heard coming from outside the starship. It said, "Give me your Starship". It could only be the voice of God. Captain Jenkins said, "What do you want with my starship?" and the voice answered, "You have been wandering my galaxy for 10 years and now you have the audacity to question me, your God." "I was going to take you back home to Earth, but now for your disobedience, you will wander the universe for all eternity!"

THE MELBOURNE CUP DREAM

The train came screaming towards the platform. It was speeding as it was running late. The train driver was on his way to Flemington Station from the outer suburbs. There were people dressed in all their race going fancy outfits. The ladies looked amazing with their Fascinators and their colourful dresses, each one outdoing the other. As the ladies walked towards the grandstand, the horses neighed in excitement and the jockeys as well. Verry Elleegant strutted past a stunning lady who wanted to pat her on the nose. The horse, 'Prince of Arran,' became jealous and wanted a pat on the nose from the lady, too. When the race began, Prince of Arran missed the start as he was thinking of the lady who patted him as being a jockey and was disappointed that he had a male jockey and nearly flipped the jockey off his back. "Oh dear, how terrible" the jockey exclaimed.

The race was in Marco's dream, days before it happened. He decided to bet on Verry Elleegant and these ladies were stuck in his head when he woke up the following morning, along with the horses.

Marco wished he was small and light in weight so he could be a jockey. He was disappointed that he had put on extra kilos in his later years. But he was good at other sports, especially cricket.

His dream to win the Melbourne Cup was once fulfilled and he wanted to feel like that again!

BUNGEE JUMPING MISHAP

On the weekend we went bungee jumping over a river. A girl jumped off the edge screaming "Aaaaa" because she was wearing a dress. "Oh no, wrong clothes choice!" she said. "I didn't mean to wear my G-string!" But the crowd above shouted back "WE LIKE YOUR choice of clothing! We think you deliberately wore your pink G-string"

GETTING DRUNK AT THE POOL

In the late Spring, there was a heatwave that made everyone lazy. At the Bondi Motel Holiday Resort everyone was trying to cool down, they jumped into the pool with cold drinks and ice-cold beer. Later in the day, they all became drunk and silly, so the lifeguard said, "Everyone OUT!" "But we LIVE here!" someone shouted back, and a streaker put his clothes back on and left the pool.

LAUGHING HYENAS

A Pride of Lions crept quietly, deep into the jungle at night, stalking the Zebras. The Lion pride's Queen and sisters tripped over a large Diamond Python, 15 metres in length. It was outraged from being woken out of its sleep and bit the Queen. The Queen shouted, "RRRROOOAAARRR!" "Oh NO, you didn't!" roared the Queen's sister. The Lion's attacked the Python and there was an enormous rumble, a Rumble in the Jungle! The Hyena just watched from a bush and laughed and laughed, as Hyenas do.

THE DEATH OF ROCK 'N' ROLL

On the first day of Spring, we heard a Budgie sing an old school rock song—I Love Rock 'n' Roll—from the top branch of a tree. Suddenly, a big buzzard swooped, misjudged the angle and crashed headfirst into the budgie and Rock 'n' Roll died. It was the Day the Music Died.

THE UFO SIGHTING

Into the darkness, I struggled to see without my night vision, but I saw in space and amongst the stars a UFO—a UFO that was about to crash land into our Earth! Later, there were reports of a crashed UFO and scientists discovering four-legged creatures inside. Some people reckoned they were half-eaten cows because Dingos were found at the UFO crash site. But others think the aliens survived and are walking the Earth today!

THE VIRUS ENDS IN A WIN

I flew to Melbourne on a plane and caught a virus! The virus was something incredible, it stopped the whole world! People were stuck in their homes like prisoners. The world was in chaos. We were watching it on television while our country was in lockdown. Melbourne went into a second lockdown, and I was trapped there! Fortunately, the lockdown eased, and I flew home to Sydney after I watched the Melbourne Cup. My horse won because there was a massive $50,000 bet on him (which was suspicious). But that is why I bet on him because I know these things can turn into winners!

THE HOT SUMMER

Last summer when the sun was hot like a bushfire, we jumped off the waterfall, naked. When we got out of the water, we saw someone had stolen our clothes! So, we had to cover ourselves with gum leaves and bark, and because our car had also been stolen, we had to hitch-hike home! We were standing on the side of the road trying to stop our gum leaves from blowing away, we were embarrassed some cars looked like they were going to stop but then sped up again and, other cars just beeped their horns and didn't stop. We were lucky when a nice old lady stopped for us and she said, "don't be embarrassed" and took us all the way home.

BUSHRES AND FLOODS

After the bushfire, the floods came and trapped animals inside houses like prisoners. The animals became depressed, so the psychiatrist prescribed them all antidepressant injections and the drug companies made more money. The animals recovered from their depression and got on with their lives.

SEARCH FOR ETERNAL YOUTH

I dreamed I was an astronaut, and I explored the galaxies. With my longevity injection, I could live 10,000 years. This enabled me to discover a planet and become its King. My people admired me like a God, and I would show them the ways of eternal youth. After four millennia I was feeling nostalgic and wanted to know what was happening with my mother Earth and my descendants. I was wondering if technology had elevated them to the stars, like I had. So, I returned to Earth, and I discovered the planet had been destroyed by an asteroid and the people had passed into eternity. My new interplanetary people went in search of the lost galaxy, Heaven. When I woke up and realised it was all a dream, I was okay with it because I had the great idea to write down the dream. To my amazement I created this story.

THE SKILL OF THE HUNT

The paratroopers were jumping off the dam, practicing manoeuvres for the new Star Wars movie. They were going to be alien invaders, projecting themselves into the galaxy with their new slingshot method projectiles. The paratroopers were excited and started filming themselves with their fancy outfits. They were swimming, pretending to hunt for the predators and fishing the great white sharks to practice the skill of the hunt, for the movie was to be called *Return of The Hunter.*

THE LIONS, KINGS OF THE JUNGLE

In the savannah in Africa, all animals fight to survive. The wildebeests are scared, for the lions are going to eat them. The lions are the kings of the jungle, they rule. Only the hyenas give them trouble. The lions are ferocious, hungry and terrorising. They go for the weakest, with the mothers protecting their babies. And sometimes the baby elephants get caught, but they do not feel the pain because they are in shock when the lions bite the back of their necks.

But lions are also majestic, brave and courageous. The rangers try to protect the lions from poachers because their numbers are dwindling. And they stay to survive like the rest of the animals.

The lions continue their domination of the jungle for they are the kings.

THE MOTHER DOG

Once there was a little boy who had a little puppy. They grew up together and had lots of fun. There was a kitten who played with the pup and they were friends. And then the pup grew up and had pups herself. And the kitten grew up and had kittens. And they were both grandparents.

The little boy grew up and had children. And his children grew up with the pups and the kittens.

One of the pups became a guide dog, the other one a guard dog and another a companion dog. And the last dog became a sniffer dog. The mother dog went to a doggie nursing home and all her pups and the cats' kittens and all the little boys' and girls' come to visit her.

And the children's children, the pups' pups and the kittens' kittens kept up the tradition of being together as a family for many many generations to come.

SPRING

I am grateful for spring and warm weather

Because you don't have to shiver as the night approaches

And the flowers look nice in the gardens.

In spring you can get a bit of sunshine in the morning

And stay out later because of daylight saving

The sunshine lasts longer and makes my depression go away

And makes me smile.

And I am thankful for spring

That makes life worth living.

THE PEST CONTROL MAN

Pests were accumulating in the house, so we brought in the pest control man. The man took out his toolbox and his spray gun. He started spraying the floor and, suddenly, I saw the cockroaches were scampering. They ran towards my feet, so I stomped on them and started dancing and singing *La Cucaracha*. I could have used the broom and swept them away but the broom wasn't nearby, fortunately, the mop was, so I mopped the cockroaches off the floor and the pest control man said, "you deserve a prize for making my job easier" and gave me a twenty-five percent discount off the bill. Years later, I found the occasional dead cockroach on the floor, and I knew he gave me a long-lasting spray and the dust mites were gone too.

THE JOLLY SANTA

Santa jumped off Rudolph's back and pulled out his sack of toys. "HO HO HO it's been a terrible year, but Christmas is finally here! My elves have been scrambling, tirelessly working from home building all these wonderful toys."

Trucks for the boys and Barbie dolls for the girls to give to all the Kindies in the schools. The teacher hugs Santa and says, "thank you Santa and all the best for the New Year". After Christmas, Santa goes on holiday for three months, and for nine months he and his elves are scrambling to make toys for the next Christmas. This time the boys will get Barbie dolls and the girls will get rocket ships, of course. Then, there was some screaming and squealing and Santa decided to give *all* the children Barbie dolls and rocket ships!

HALLOWEEN SPECIAL

The Big Dipper came screaming past and I dropped my ice-cream on the ground. The roller coaster was very scary! The smaller roller coaster was full of people because they liked a bit of a thrill and not too much scariness. The ghost train was full of teenagers because they liked the thrill of being scared. The ghosts were not that scary, but the zombies were. The zombies had blood in their mouths and one bit the vampire on the neck. The blood was fake of course, as were the zombies, and the magician pulled a rabbit out of a hat and that was skilful. He also cut four women in half and put the wrong bodies back together and they became zombies. The magician act was the highlight of the theme park and the zombies and ghosts weren't real, but everyone thought they were, then four teenage girls were screaming with excitement, saying, "We were scared but it was really fun! When is there going to be another one?" The magician replied, "every Halloween, it's a Halloween special but you can look forward to the Mardi Gras special, very soon."

THE TIME MACHINE

In the Middle Ages, way back when the Knights were jousting, we were observing from our Time Machine. We saw a horse get hit in the chest by a jousting spear and fall over, and the reserve horse next in line ran away. Then, we saw a Chariot Race from The Roman Empire, and we saw the Egyptian slaves building the Pyramids. We went to the future and saw a colony on the Moon. They were building the New World because the Earth was about to expire due to Global Warming. Then, we went further into the future and saw them building train tracks on Mars using slaves because they had overthrown the Martians and enslaved them. We didn't like this, it looked like a horror movie, so we decided to go back to our own time. And we landed smack bang in the middle of Frangipani House. Then, we decided to destroy our Time Machine because of the nightmares it gave us.

THE CYCLONE CATASTROPHE

Remember when we went to the new Westfield shopping centre, a huge horse was dangling from the ceiling, which was made from old wood collected from a tree recently uprooted during the cyclone catastrophe that had not been forecast. Westfield's insurance company refused to pay for the damage to the heritage tree because of some technicalities. Westfield turned a negative into a positive by their ingenious architect/artist and designer who created an artwork out of the damaged tree.

HAVE A GOOD EXPERIENCE AT THE TAB

The horses run faster when the big money is on.

The horses try harder when they like their jockey.

No one wants to come last.

Everyone wants to come first.

But there can be only one winner. Who will it be?

After the race, no matter if you have won or lost

You will still have money to bet with and another chance to win.

The experience of betting is better than being lonely and bored and we all like to win.

It is better to be happy and challenging your mind,

Than be depressed and have dementia,

With one hundred thousand in the bank.

Just make sure you have food to eat and pay the rent.

And I am thankful when the horses win for me.

THE HORSE, THE ZEBRA, THE DONKEY AND THE MULE

He yelled, 'Liar!"

The horse and zebra were racing each other, and the zebra won.

"How could the Zebra win against the horse?" Marco asked.

"His stripes were painted on!" Someone replied.

"A Zebra can't win a race against a horse," a third guy said.

"Let's check! That was not a horse, it was a donkey! Or a mule at best!" Marco yelled.

"Zebras run from lions. They have to be fast!" the owner of the zebra said.

They checked. Finally, he was a horse with stripes painted on and the other horse was a Mule.

And all bets were cancelled.

THE UNSTABLE SUMMER

On a scorching hot summer's day when the temperature was forty-seven degrees, and everyone was screaming out for a cool change, there was a sudden crack of thunder and lightning as clouds covered the sky. The lightning bolt hit the clock at twenty past three. There was a splishing and a splashing at the pool, then came the deluge of rain and made everyone outside the pool wetter than the people inside the pool! The cry for a cool change had happened with a twenty-degree drop, and forty-seven turned into twenty-seven. Then, the fiery sun poked his head out and blasted everyone with forty-seven-degree heat again! And everyone complained about the heat until the evening when the temperature lowered to twenty-two degrees and stayed like that for three days. Singlets turned into jackets and everyone said, "is it summer or is it winter? These up and down days!"

BETTER THAN THREE BIRDS WITH ONE STONE

It was midnight when the full moon shone bright, the Wolf and Owl were howling together. Then came the Giraffe and nudged the Owl because he liked his tune. The Owl said, "why do you bother me?" "I'm telling on you to the Wolf." The Wolf came and ate the Giraffe, and then came a Lion and ate the Wolf and then a Crocodile came and tore the Lion apart. Then the Hippopotamus waddled up and swallowed the Crocodile with his big mouth and said, "I am the King" and the Game Hunter came and shot the Hippopotamus and said, "I am the Boss" and pulled out all the animals from the Hippopotamus's stomach. First, he pulled out the Crocodile and then the Lion, then the Wolf and lastly the Giraffe. He laughed and said, "I've done much better than Killing Three Birds with One Stone." And, the Owl flew away, with a flurry of feathers, and said, "You didn't kill me!"

MARCO'S FANCY PET NAMES

Wendy and I wanted some animal pet company, so we went to the pet shop and bought two cats and two guinea pigs. We named the cats Qwatie and Kootzicoo, and we named the guinea pigs Luwishie and Proop Proop. When we got home, we went to sleep and the cats fought over their names, and so did the guinea pigs.

Qwatie called out to Kootzicoo, "I've got a better name than you" and Kootzicoo said, "No, I'm the best because Marco named me Kootzicoo first." And Luwishie said, "I've got the best guinea pig name. Wendy called me that first."

We found a mouse under the TV and the cats wanted to keep him as a pet. We didn't know whether he was a mouse or a rat because he was so big, so we called him Big Mig. And I said, "Kootzicoo has got the best name because I thought of it first."

PLORJASOM'S BATTLE

Plorjasom wanted to copyright his name so that it would not be stolen, but he could not work out how to spell it.

Plorjasom said to himself if I don't know how to spell something, I'll spell it so that I can understand it. Plorjasom was upset because he made up the name Skylander and somebody stole it, and he didn't get any money for it.

Plorjasom was fuming because they plagiarised him. Plorjasom wrote a book of funny stories, and in the last story, he told everyone that he made up the name "Skylander."

Plorjasom's book of funny stories made the world laugh. He became famous and forgot all about the plagiarising of Skylander.

Now Plorjasom stories are complete, and he wants the world to know that his real name is Marco. He has forgiven the people who plagiarised Skylander, on this day, February 1, National Day of Forgiveness.

PEGASUS

ALIEN VISITATION

The aliens visited Earth and their flying saucers were visible to many people. The aliens looked like lizards standing upright with long legs and a short tail. People wanted to fight the aliens, so they put on their boxing gloves and tried to punch them! But the aliens were too evasive, and no one could land a punch. The aliens said, "We come in peace. We are looking for a planet to co-inhabit because our planet is overpopulated." Then the President said, "Why don't you discover a planet and claim it for yourselves and live there?". The aliens replied, "that would take too much work and involve slavery to build a world from an empty planet." So, the President said, "What can you offer us to allow you to cohabit with us?" The aliens replied, "We can offer you gold." The President said, "Go back home and bring back 100 kg of gold." The aliens agreed and, when they flew off in their flying saucer a fair distance from Earth, the President ordered the Air Force to shoot them down with a missile. But the missile missed the saucers because the aliens are good at evasion. Then, another four missiles were dispatched and the flying saucer, in its attempts to evade the missiles, crashed into the Empire State Building. The President was criticised by the Opposition, who said, "You should have let them bring the 100 kg gold!" There was an election the following year and the President said in his statement, "Do you really believe they would have bought back 100 kg of gold?" and that was the statement that won him the election and the Opposition looked like fools.

THE BIRTHDAY CAKE

Wendy walked into the kitchen and saw her dog, Butch, rolling around on the floor. He had a full stomach and chocolate icing on his nose. Wendy remembered the cake she had baked for her daughter's twenty-first birthday. It was missing from the kitchen table. The plate was on the floor and the trail of cake crumbs led to the dog.

"Oh, no! What have you done Butch!" Wendy screamed. Because of the hysteria the dog ran out of the kitchen, whimpering, squealing, and barking. At that moment, Marco arrived in a fancy car. He stepped out holding a large cake three times bigger than the cake Wendy had made.

"Don't blame the dog, Wendy. This is a cake I bought for Emma's birthday. I gave the other cake to the dog because I wanted to impress you with this big cake for Emma's birthday said Marco. Wendy was so happy that she gave Marco a big hug. When Emma arrived home from college, they told her that Wendy had made the cake, and everyone was happy. And the dog entered the room wagging his tail.

A SUDDEN SURPRISE

I wish I could paint landscapes and seascapes again. I remember when I was a teenager, I used to paint landscapes and seascapes every weekend, in the lounge room. On the dining table, I used my oil paints and copied them from a book. I did not paint any animals except a horse eating the grass in one of my seascapes of a lighthouse. The horse was not in the original painting, I just added the horse to make the picture more interesting. I remember my brother was jealous of my artistic ability, he got a brush with paint and poked me in the face with it. So, I went into the garage and opened a tin of house paint and, with a large house brush, I snuck up on my brother and tapped him on the shoulder and slapped him in the face with the brush full of blue paint. Then, I dropped the brush on the concrete, and he chased me around the house, but he didn't catch me. I told him, "Don't touch my paintings or brushes or I will pour the tin of house paint on your head!" I helped him wash the paint off his face. He said, "That slap in the face was a sudden surprise!" And I said, "You deserved it!"

THE TIGER'S ADVENTURE

Saboo, The Tiger was running through the shopping centre because he escaped from the circus display that was on the ground floor. He was a slippen' and a slidden' on smooth tiles because his claws couldn't get a grip. Oh, boy was this Tiger hungry! So, he kept running until the smell of chicken entered his nostrils and he found the chicken shop. The shoppers were terrified because they didn't know The Tiger was tame, so they screamed in panic and scattered to the four corners of the building. The shopkeeper of the Charcoal Chicken store acted instinctively and threw The Tiger a chicken so he wouldn't attack anyone. While Saboo The Tiger was munching on the chicken, Marco, The Big Cat and Lion Tamer shot him with a tranquilizer dart because the police threatened to shoot The Tiger dead. Marco went to check The Tiger was asleep, then his assistants, Wendy, and Paul, put The Tiger on a stretcher and carried him back to the cage on the truck so that he could be transported back to Tiger Training School at The Circus.

A SHOCKING INSIGHT INTO MARCO'S STORYTELLING

The electricity was convulsing through someone's brain as I woke up and realised, I was next in line. I knew that I was next unless I said "No." I did say "No" but they told me that I needed it and it would help with my depression and it would be the last one. So, I said "Okay."

The electricity was silent, and I could not remember my dream properly it was like I had lightning in my brain, and I was dancing through a corridor of thunder and lightning.

My depression went away, and I was ready to be discharged from hospital. The memory of the hospital admission was a little bit foggy but then my memory cleared up and I realised why they gave me the shock treatment.

Some years later, my memory improved and got even better and that is why I am able to write this story because my memory is excellent, and my intellectual ability is on 'high.'

Occasionally, I write stories—a few from life experiences—but mostly I invent them out of nothing. I also get ideas from other people and write them down and create a story from that. I believe my story writing is unique—a cross between a poem and a story, and some are like jokes written in poetic form. I like people to read my stories and tell me what they think.

Epilogue:
Electric shock treatment (ECT) won't give you story writing abilities, but it can cure severe depression.

THE BIG FORWARDS WILL COLLIDE

The Rugby League trials are underway, and an underdog beats the favourite and it's all for confidence because when the real games start, there will be collisions and thumping, and fast running and the big men will collide, and the small men will throw the ball thirty metres and the kickers will kick the ball sixty metres and the Wingers will chase the ball and score in the corner and the Full-Backs will make tri-saving tackles. When the semi-finals arrive, the intensity will step up another level. The big Forward will collide with a thump and get the pass away to a little Half-Back and then pass to a Five-Eight who will step the Opposition's Centre and pass to his Centre and then the Full-Back who will give it to the Winger who will score in the corner, and the Goal Kicker will have to convert the try from the sideline to win the game in front of a capacity crowd. All the pressure is on the Goal Kicker, either he is a Hero or a Loser because the winner goes into the Grand Final. When the Grand Final comes everyone knows it is a Grand Final because the intensity is one hundred percent and everything is faster and the action is suspenseful and when a team comes from behind to win with a sensational try and conversion from the sideline to win a thriller, that is a spectacle that's fitting for a Grand Final and won't be forgotten for another year.

THE DRAGON SLAYER

Once upon a time, there was a magical land that had a mythical dragon who lived in an undersea cave. He could swim as well as fly and breathe fire, so he was a clever beast but not friendly.

He would breathe his fire on the houses and then watch the people scramble to put out the fires. Then he would fly away and laugh and a tree would be set ablaze. The fire horses would come with their carts and barrels of water but no one could kill this terrible fire-breathing beast—until the Hero arrived and he said "I'm the Dragon Slayer."

The next time the Dragon arrived to burn down a house, the Dragon Slayer was waiting and shot him with a spear in the side of the neck. The fireman sprayed the Dragon in the mouth and extinguished his fire. The Dragon Slayer cut off the Dragon's head with his big sword with an act of courage and the Dragon was dead.

The villagers slept easy that night, but...back in the Dragon's Lair, there was an egg and it cracked open and the little Dragon poked its head out. The Dragon Slayer's wife gave birth to a little baby boy and they called him Junior.

ITALY MEETS AUSTRALIA

Angelo and Luigi stepped off the plane and were greeted by Duncan and Wally. Duncan and Wally said, "Welcome to Australia" and, Luigi said, "What about Giuseppe? He is straggling behind with his walking stick". Giuseppe said, "Let's go to a restaurant and eat a big plate of spaghetti" and Wally asked, "What about a pizza?" Angelo replied, "A pizza will be delicious". Duncan said, "Let's stop at the Pub for a few beers first". Angelo replied, "Yeah, I'd love to have a beer with Duncan".

At the Pub, there was a TAB and Luigi said, "Look there's Marco having a bet on the horses". Marco said, "There's a horse named Antonio Giuseppe, do you want to bet on him Luigi? He's 28 to 1, a good ruffe". Josh, who was with Marco said, "Look at this horse who is called High Fly Marco, he is 44 to 1. He's an even bigger ruffe. What a good rough chance he is".

Luigi, Giuseppe, Angelo, Wally and Duncan all bet on $20 each on Antonio Giuseppe. Marco and Josh had a secret bet and would not tell anyone what it was because they wanted to win more money without dividing the winnings.

When the race was on, Antonio Giuseppe missed the start and came out last. High Fly Marco was leading the race all the way, he went out 20 lengths in front in a 2000m race, but with 400m to go, he started to get tired, and Antonio Giuseppe was coming quickly behind him and, Luigi called out his horse, "Antonio Giuseppe! Antonio Giuseppe!" and, Josh called out, "Marco! High Fly Marco! High Fly Marco!" Marco kept silent because he wasn't going to call out his own name.

With 20m to go, it was neck and neck between the two ruffes. High Fly Marco put in extra burst of effort, even though he was tired, because he wanted to win, after leading all the way. And, right on the line Antonio Giuseppe lunged at the finishing post and, it was a photo finish.

When the photo was shown it was declared a dead heat and, Josh and Marco were cheering and shouted, "We've got the quinella 10 times each!" and, when the quinella dividend was shown, it was $485. Marco and Josh both won $4850 each. Marco said, "Right, that does it! We're getting a limousine to the Motel and we're going to eat Lasagne, Pizza and Gelato. And, Wendy said, "I want to come too, and I'm staying with Marco tonight".

ELIYA AND ELENORE THE TRUMPETING ELEPHANTS

In the Middle Ages, along the Nile River stomped Eliya the Elephant, with his girlfriend Elenore, by his side. "I'm angry, my hunger fuels my anger" trumpeted Eliya. Elenore said, "They are exploiting us, they make us carry large rocks and don't feed us enough. We need to get out of here, we need to break free. Let's all get out of here and make a stampede" so, they both started stomping and trumpeting, and trumpeting and stomping. They made so much noise, that the guards though it was a thunderstorm. But then they realised that the elephants were having a revolution. The guards were terrified and unleashed the Lions on them. But instead, the Lions ate the guards. The Lions jumped onto a raft and the Elephants pushed the raft across the river to the jungle on the other side. And the Lions and the Elephants walked off into the sunset, and Eliya kissed Elenore on the trunk.

THE LION WHO LEARNED TO BE TAME

Luiwishie the grey-haired, balding lion (who was not quite middle-aged yet) is stressed and grumpy. He is losing his hair, and going grey, and prowling up and down in his cage in Taronga Park Zoo. "Grr", growled Luiwishie, "I don't get enough freedom to run, I don't get enough food to eat, and the elephants get a big enclosure and get to give children rides on their backs!"

Luiwishie wonders if he could be tame, and play with the elephants and the children, or if he would eat them. Mayoog the Monkey could see Luiwishie's distress and felt sorry for him.

"Hey Luiwishie, if you weren't so grumpy, and smile some more, they'd let you out of the cage to play with the elephants and the children. When the zookeeper comes to feed you, smile and purr like a kitten!"

Later that day, the zookeeper came by with Luiwishie's dinner. Luiwishie started to smile, and purr like a little kitten, and rolled over onto his back to show his belly. The zookeeper decided to let Luiwishie play with the elephants and the children. Luiwishie walked over to the elephants and started to purr, and the elephant was pleased and kissed Luiwishie on the head with his trunk. The children hugged Luiwishie and patted him on the head, and Luiwishie was happy!

A STORY MADE OUT OF NOTHING

Melissa the Marvellous Dolphin, Megan the Miraculous Marsupial Wallaby, Athena the Awesome Architect, Greg the Giraffe and Marco the Magnificent and Amazing author: were trying to think of ways to write a story, something that would be: Funny, Amazing, and Ironic, they would like to think of all three of them (but to be honest even one would do).

Melissa swam swiftly towards Megan the Marsupial Wallaby and whispered in her ear, something about water and sunshine -------

Athena said "How about Byron Bay? I went on a holiday and it was beautiful! Byron Bay had beautiful dolphins" – "Yeah I like to swim with my own kind!" Shouted Melissa the Dolphin with excitement.

Greg the Giraffe stretched out his long neck and said, "I'm not gonna nudge another owl while he's hooting because he might tell on me to the wolf!"

Marco said: "Sounds like a story brewing in my mind, I need to put this all together, it's like a jigsaw puzzle, or connect the dots. Somehow I gotta create this story and maybe I will meet a beautiful lady and tell her my stories!"

Megan the Marsupial Wallaby climbed on Greg the Giraffes back and said, "Take me to Marco, he's swimming with Melissa the Dolphin and Athena".

When Megan got there, she overheard the conversation between Marco and Athena. "I'm an amazing architect, I specialise in designing houses, but how can I help you design a story!" said Athena. "You thought of Byron Bay you can think of anything," said Marco.

"Look, all of you shut up! You keep saying you will write a story but none of you are coming up with ideas, you just keep repeating the same thing over and over again and you aren't creating anything!" everyone was stunned into silence by the fury of this seemingly innocent Marsupial, Megan.

"You know what, you are right, writing stories is too hard, because all the creative ideas in the world are gone, even the Beatles didn't write 100 hits. Let's just order a pizza and go watch the chariot races at the TAB" – Marco said. "SOUNDS GREAT!" Replied everyone.

So Marco was unable to write anything new and interesting for the first time in his life, it was just another boring ordinary day when a Dolphin, Giraffe, Author, Architect and a Wallaby eating Pizza at the TAB while watching Chariot Races.

CPSIA information can be obtained
at www.ICGtesting.com
Printed in the USA
LVHW071605020721
691771LV00009B/285

9 780228 854067